DOCTOR DOLITTLE

CONTENTS

"Doctor Dolittle" -
On Stage & Screen

Leslie Bricusse outside the Apollo Theatre, London, home of "Doctor Dolittle."

Early in 1965, Hollywood film producer Arthur P. Jacobs, popularly known in the trade as Apjac, called me in London to say that he was planning to make a major musical movie based on Hugh Lofting's "Doctor Dolittle" stories, and if invited, would I be interested to write it? … Would I be interested?

The plan had been for the film to re-unite the legendary Lerner & Loewe with Rex Harrison, but for various reasons of health and schedule, Lerner & Loewe had passed on the project, although Rex was still keen on the idea. Apjac had put forward my name to Darryl Zanuck, whose son Richard was the new young head of production at Twentieth Century Fox, as an alternative writer, on the not very convincing premise that I was planning to write another musical based on perhaps the most famous of all animal stories, "Noah's Ark."

Long story short, a few weeks later, at a meeting in San Francisco, my childhood Hollywood dream came true, and I was given the mammoth triple assignment as screenwriter, composer and lyricist for this enormously complex motion picture.

I had no illusions about the fact that, for the first few months, Rex was considerably less than enchanted – and who could blame him?" - to be offered me as a replacement for the fabled Lerner & Loewe.

Wonderfully cantankerous, and delighting in his wickedness, Rex was also a highly amusing man and a comedic actor of rare calibre, and out of our shaky start was born a firm friendship that was to continue until the end of his life.

The rest of the cast and production team were, together and separately, a joy to work with – both Zanucks, director Richard Fleischer, choreographer Herb Ross, and Rex's three co-star actors, Anthony Newley, Samantha Eggar and Richard Attenborough, all of whom, happily, were old friends of mine. We had a lot of fun together, taking turns to deal with the quicksilver moods of the regularly wrathful Rex.

Leslie Bricusse with Rex Harrison, the screen star of "Doctor Dolittle."

I particularly had to battle him for many months to keep the first song I'd written for him, "Talk To The Animals," in the score.

"It's such a silly song," he complained. I pointed out that "Doctor Dolittle" was a children's story and he would not be judged as Henry Higgins singing it. "I should bloody well hope not," he grumbled.

Only when the song was finally filmed did Rex grudgingly concede that it was "all right." Even when "Talk To The Animals" won the Academy Award for Best Song the following year, he still retained lingering doubts about it. "Of Courseros" does not rhyme with "rhinoceros," he sniffed. And he's probably right.

It goes without saying that for years the thought of "Dolittle" as a stage musical was lurking at the back of my mind. The same thing had happened when we made the film of "Victor/Victoria," starring Julie Andrews. Writer-director Blake Edwards, composer Henry Mancini and I were well aware that in Julie we had one of the greatest musical theatre stars in history. It took us over a decade, but the show finally opened on Broadway in 1995. It was a long swim, but ultimately a triumphant one. As I write, there are more than a half-a-dozen productions of the show running or due to open around the planet.

"Dolittle" was even more difficult, because I had no idea of how to overcome the seemingly insurmountable problem of creating convincingly realistic animals for the theatre.

Some years ago, at the height of his glittering era as James Bond, I accompanied Roger Moore to Elstree Studios, where he gave a delightful rendition of "Talk To The Animals" on "The Muppet Show." We had lunch with Jim Henson and Frank Oz, the show's brilliant creators, and Jim mooted the idea of "Doctor Dolittle" in the theatre. I said that, charming and funny as I thought it would be, children needed to believe that the animals were real, and not puppets.

Leslie Bricusse with Polynesia the Parrot and Julie Andrews, who provided her voice.

Little could I have imagined then the miraculous advent of animatronic animals, and that one day I would be sitting in the biggest theatre in London, as I recently was, looking at nearly one hundred incredibly realistic animals, created by the Jim Henson Creature Shop, run by Jim's son Brian, populating the stage version of "Doctor Dolittle," and that my wife, my son, and I would be sitting, once again with our old chum Roger Moore, at the first night of "Doctor Dolittle" watching their magic unfold.

Leslie Bricusse with Mia Farrow a friend at 20th Century Fox Studios at the start of filming "Doctor Dolittle."

The icing on the cake came when Julie Andrews – Mary Poppins herself – agreed to provide the many voices of Dolittle's tutor, friend and mentor, Polynesia the parrot – a task she accomplished both brilliantly and hilariously. The wonderful and funny hours we spent together evolving Polynesia in a series of recording sessions were for me one of the unforgettable highlights of the rehearsal period.

I'll tell you what's wonderful about the theatre. I was looking at the Monday May 18th Rehearsal Call Sheet. It read simply "Rehearse Penguins – please bring tap shoes."

Isn't that great? We're all still children.

"Doctor Dolittle" in America.

During the four years (1998-2001) that "Doctor Dolittle" ran in the U.K., it was seen by many visitors from the United States, including a number of theatre producers with an eye to taking the show across the pond.

Leslie Bricusse with Tommy Tune in Lake Tahoe, Nevada.

Four years, several structural and many artistic changes, and innumerable Trans-Atlantic trips later, thanks mainly to the great Jimmy Nederlander and the head of the Pittsburgh Civic Light Opera, Van Kaplan, the show finally opened in Pittsburgh, Pennsylvania, in the summer of 2005, at the start of a major national tour. After a few months, nine-time Tony Award-winning Tommy Tune, the multi-faceted Broadway star, actor, singer, choreographer and director, stepped into the title role with his customary panache to make the show his own.

Today, exactly eight years after the show started its London rehearsals, I am happy to report that "Doctor Dolittle" is still in tune, and Tune is still in "Doctor Dolittle." Long may it be so. I have also just learned, with delight, that a new British production of "Dolittle" will open in London in 2007.

Leslie Bricusse
London, April 4, 2006

MY FRIEND THE DOCTOR

Words and Music by
LESLIE BRICUSSE

Moderate march tempo

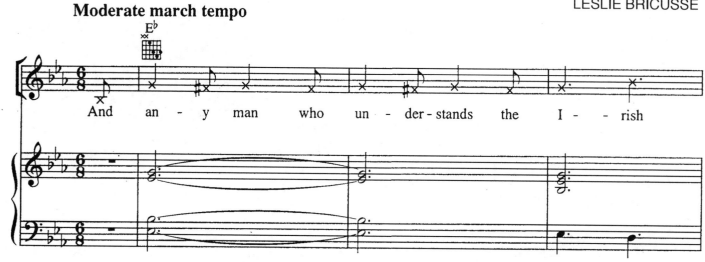

And an - y man who un - der - stands the I - rish

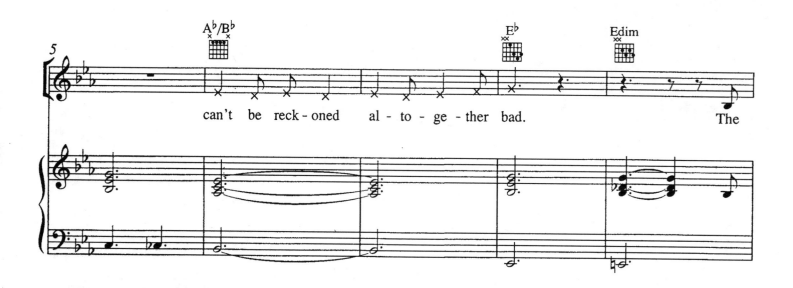

can't be reck - oned al - to - ge - ther bad. The

same way that a lu - na - tic whose pa - tron saint is Pa - ter - ick

My Friend the Doctor - 12 - 1
24491

12

THE VEGETARIAN

Words and Music by
LESLIE BRICUSSE

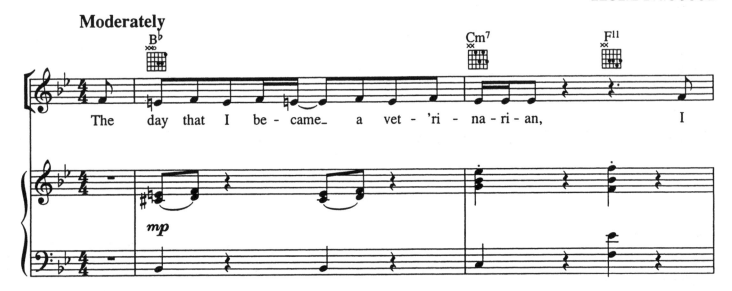

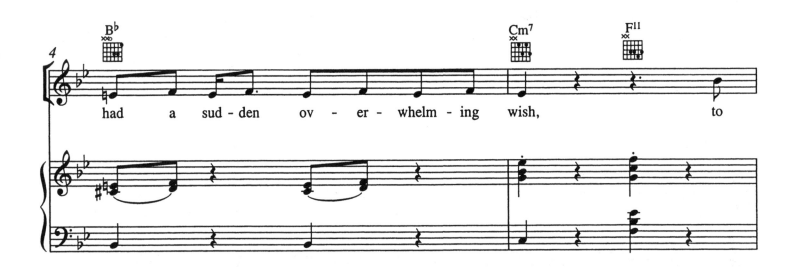

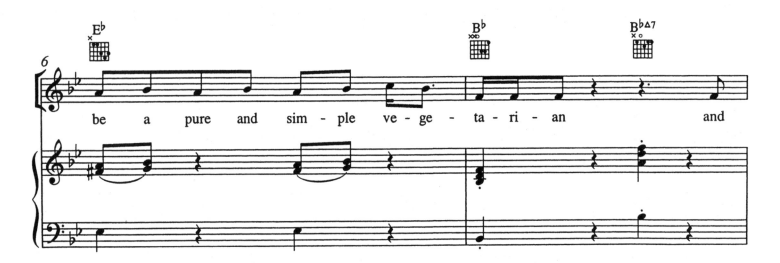

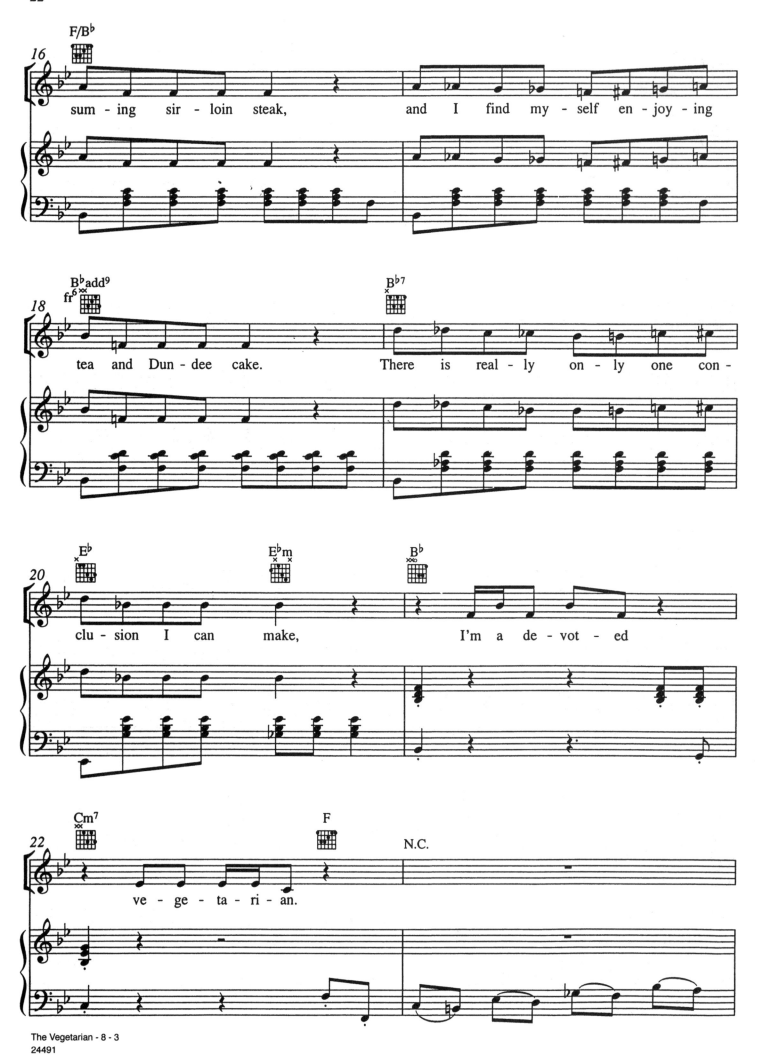

TALK TO THE ANIMALS

Words and Music by
LESLIE BRICUSSE

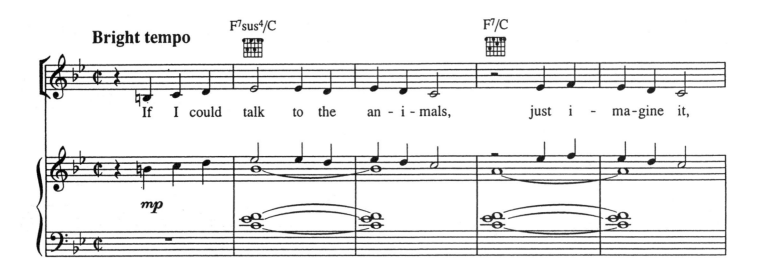

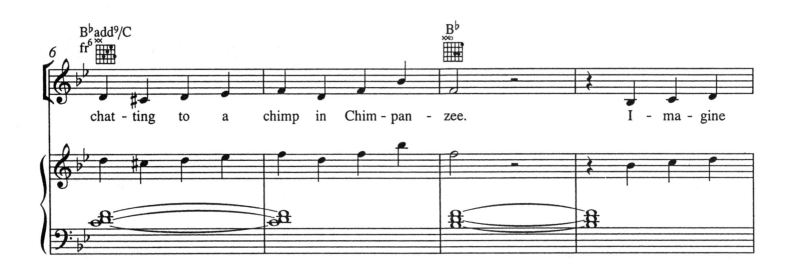

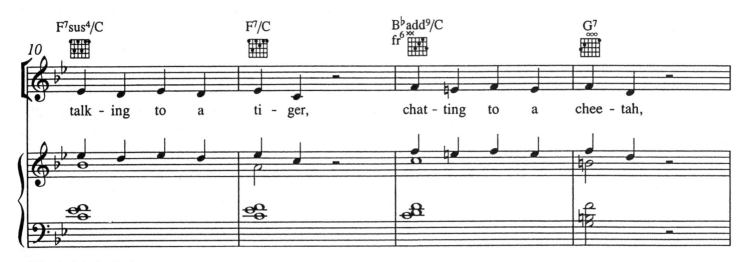

Talk to the Animals - 12 - 1
24491

34

DOCTOR DOLITTLE

Words and Music by
LESLIE BRICUSSE

Easy swing

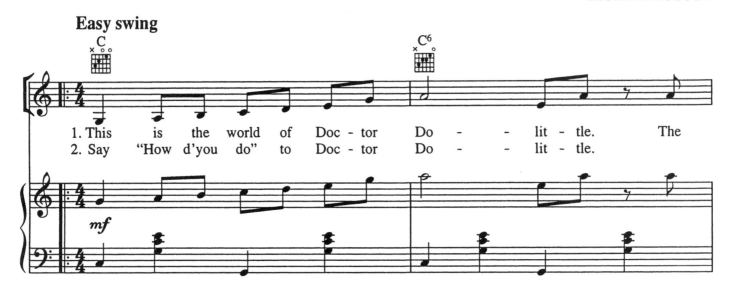

1. This is the world of Doc - tor Do - - lit - tle. The
2. Say "How d'you do" to Doc - tor Do - - lit - tle.

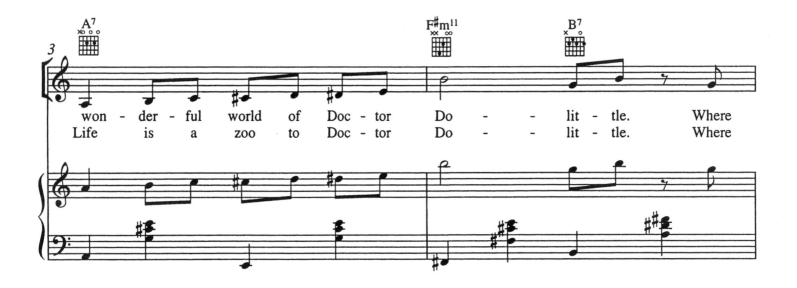

won - der - ful world of Doc - tor Do - - lit - tle. Where
Life is a zoo to Doc - tor Do - - lit - tle. Where

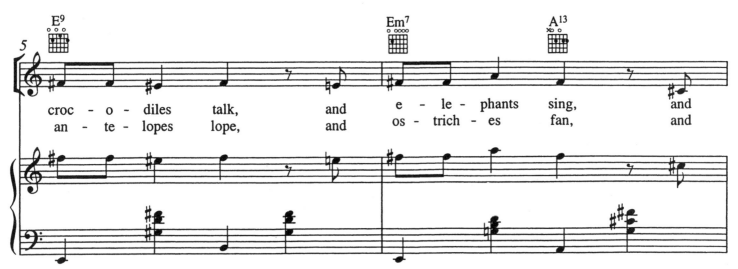

croc - o - diles talk, and e - le - phants sing, and
an - te - lopes lope, and os - trich - es fan, and

Doctor Dolittle - 6 - 1
24491

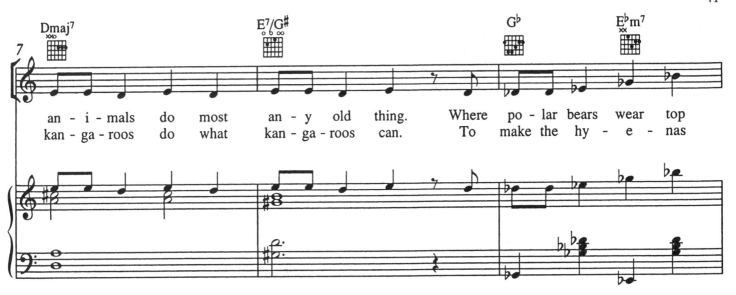

an - i - mals do most an - y old thing. Where po - lar bears wear top
kan - ga - roos do what kan - ga - roos can. To make the hy - e - nas

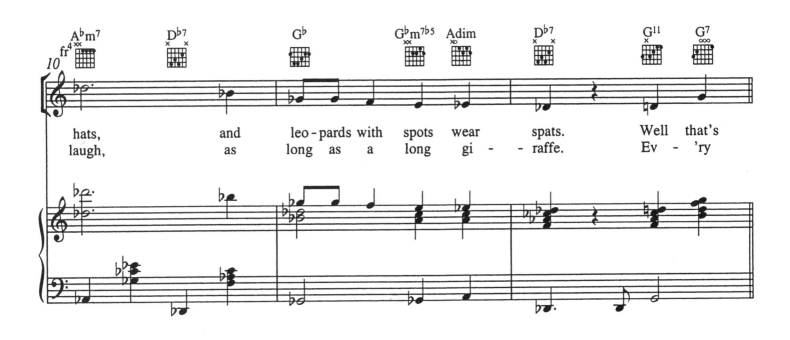

hats, and leo - pards with spots wear spats. Well that's
laugh, as long as a long gi - - raffe. Ev - 'ry

life in the world of Doc - tor Do - - lit - tle.
calf starts to moo when they see Do - - lit - tle.

Doctor Dolittle - 6 - 2
24491

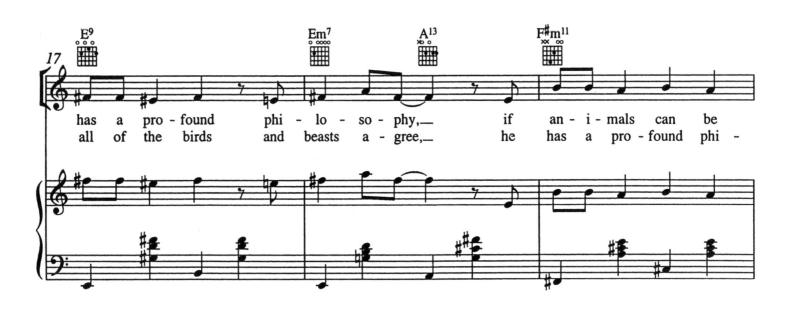

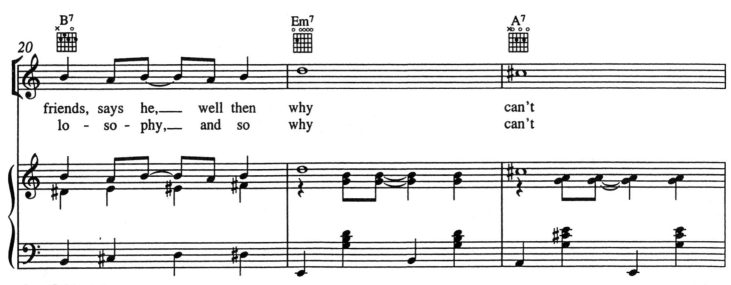

YOU'RE IMPOSSIBLE!

Words and Music by
LESLIE BRICUSSE

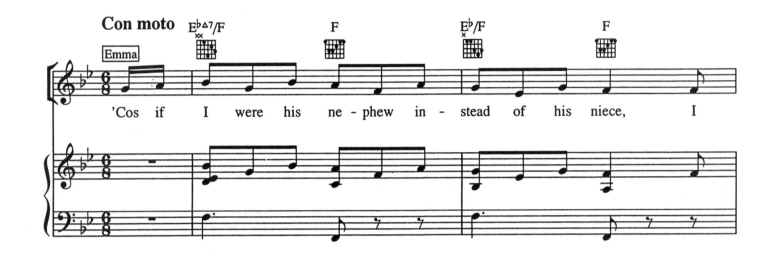

'Cos if I were his ne-phew in-stead of his niece, I

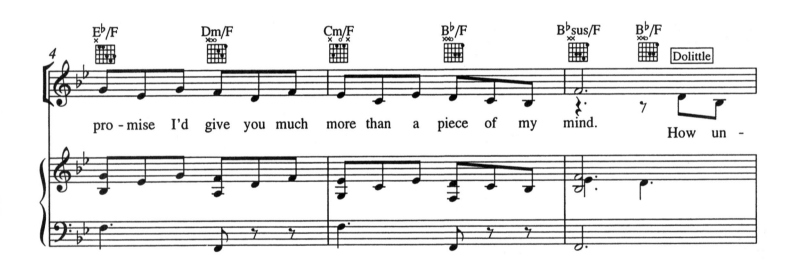

pro-mise I'd give you much more than a piece of my mind. How un-

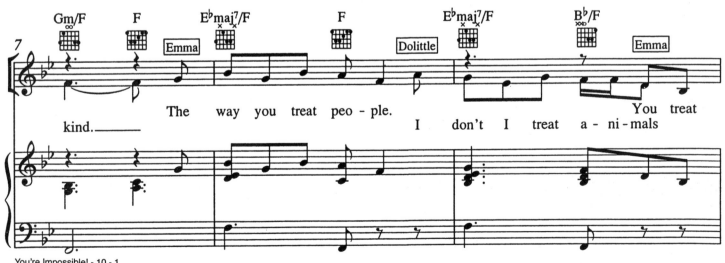

The way you treat peo-ple. You treat
kind._____ I don't I treat a-ni-mals

You're Impossible! - 10 - 1
24491

48

I'VE NEVER SEEN ANYTHING LIKE IT

Words and Music by
LESLIE BRICUSSE

Bright tempo

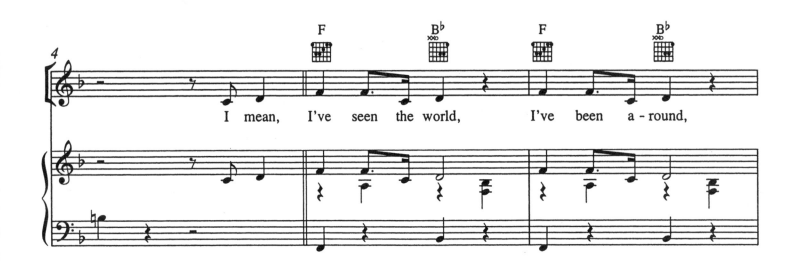

I mean, I've seen the world, I've been a-round,

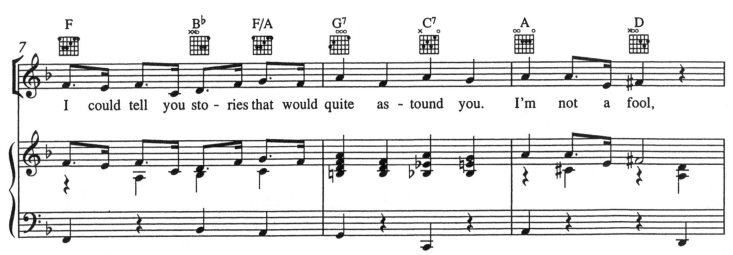

I could tell you sto - ries that would quite as - tound you. I'm not a fool,

60
A♭m7
fr4
D♭7
G♭
E♭m7
A♭m7
fr4
D♭7
63
F/C
G7
F/C
G7
67
F/C
Dm7
G7
B♭/C
C7
F
71
Gm7
Gm#7
B♭/C
C
I thought I'd seen ev - - 'ry won - der in the

64

five! 'Cos I've ne - ver seen an - y - thing

like it that's a - live. Push - mi Pull - yus are re -

mark - a - ble crea - tures, of all God's an - i - mals, they're the cle - ver - est.

They de - vel - op these re - mark - a - ble fea - tures run - ning up and down Mount

Lyrics:

dance. I mean, what can you say, what can you do?

I knew right a-way that folks will pay to view it. I said to Ted,

'Ted, lad' I said, 'This thing's the big-gest thing since home-made bread.'

Home-made bread. Home-made bread. To get that Push-mi

I've Never Seen Anything Like It - 17 - 12
24491

68

Pull - yu I'm pre - pared to sell the wife! (Spoken: Only joking Gertie!) 'Cos he's

nev - er seen an - y - thing like it in his life._____ No, I've

ne - ver seen an - y - thing like it. Ne - ver seen an - y - thing

like it, I've ne - ver seen an - y - thing like it,

I've Never Seen Anything Like It - 17 - 13
24491

—Original Drawings—

BEAUTIFUL THINGS

Words and Music by
LESLIE BRICUSSE

Flowing

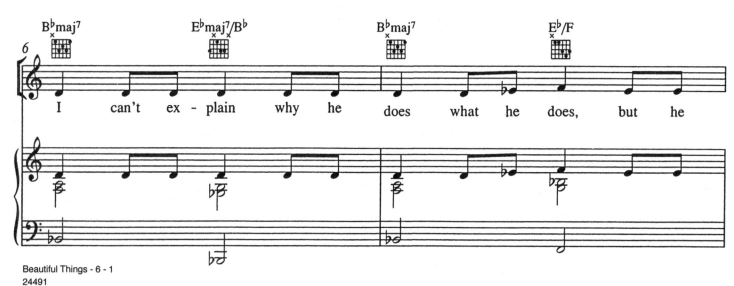

Beautiful Things - 6 - 1
24491

WHEN I LOOK IN YOUR EYES

Words and Music by
LESLIE BRICUSSE

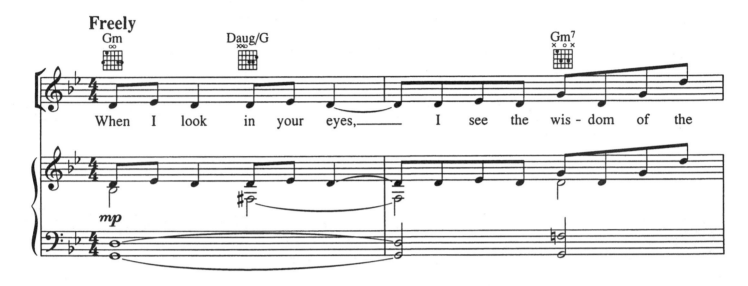

When I look in your eyes,_____ I see the wis-dom of the

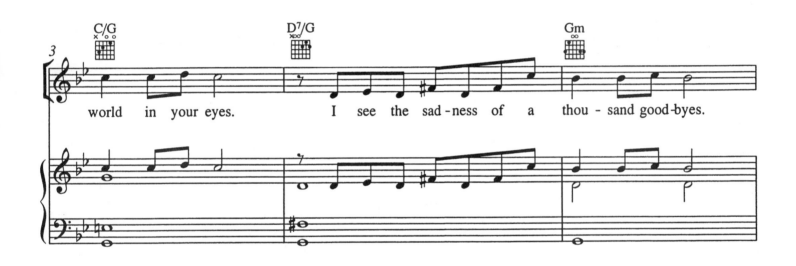

world in your eyes. I see the sad-ness of a thou-sand good-byes.

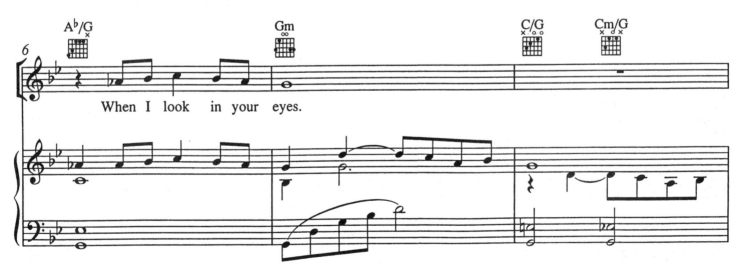

When I look in your eyes.

When I Look in Your Eyes - 4 - 1
24491

LIKE ANIMALS

Words and Music by
LESLIE BRICUSSE

Like Animals - 12 - 1
24491

95

AFTER TODAY

Words and Music by
LESLIE BRICUSSE

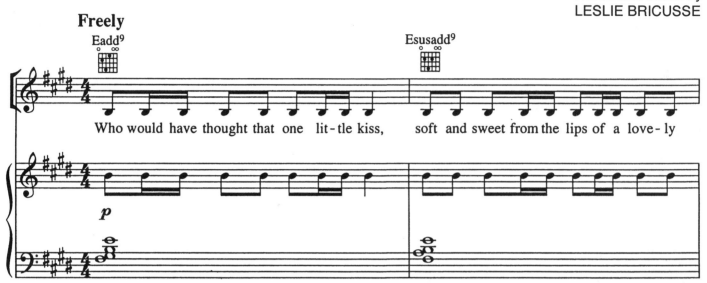

Who would have thought that one lit-tle kiss, soft and sweet from the lips of a love-ly

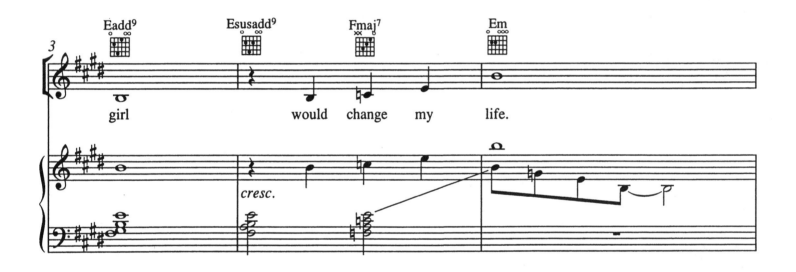

girl would change my life.

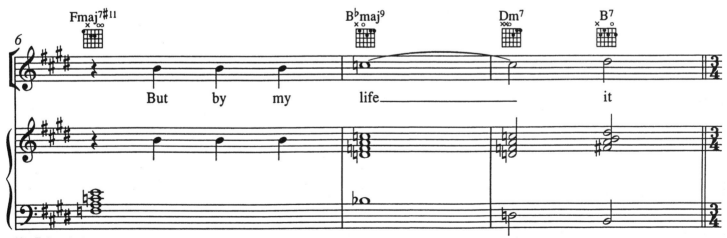

But by my life_____ it

FABULOUS PLACES

Words and Music by
LESLIE BRICUSSE

Bright waltz tempo

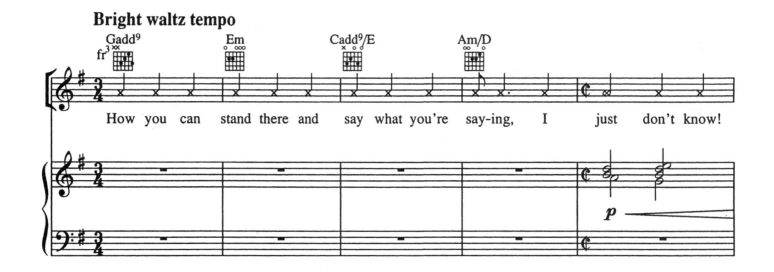

How you can stand there and say what you're say-ing, I just don't know!

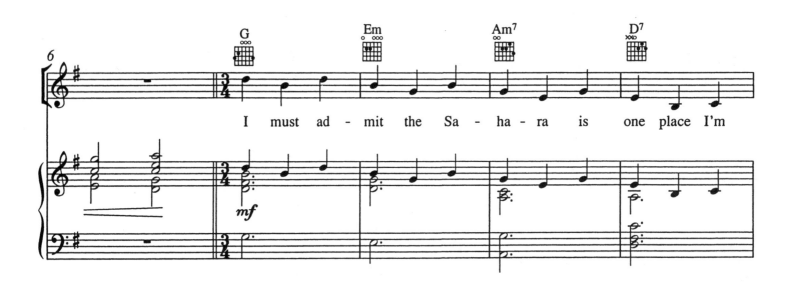

I must ad - mit the Sa - ha - ra is one place I'm

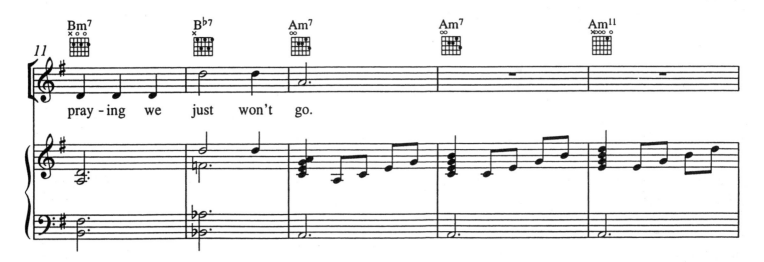

pray - ing we just won't go.

Fabulous Places - 14 - 1
24491

106

WHERE ARE THE WORDS?

Words and Music by
LESLIE BRICUSSE

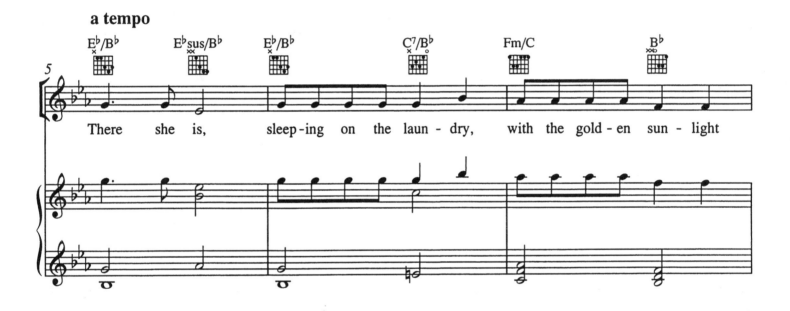

There she is, sleep-ing on the laun-dry, with the gold-en sun-light

in her hair. There's my heart, with her on the laun-dry.

Where Are the Words? - 8 - 1
24491

I THINK I LIKE YOU

Words and Music by
LESLIE BRICUSSE

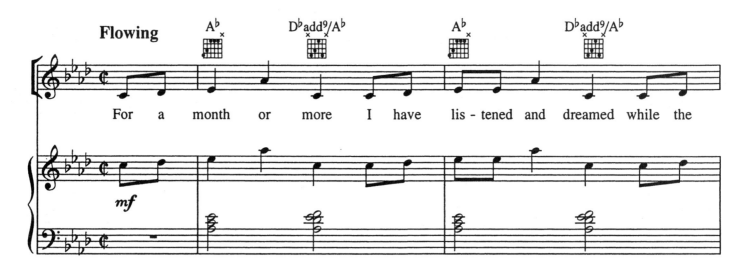

For a month or more I have lis-tened and dreamed while the

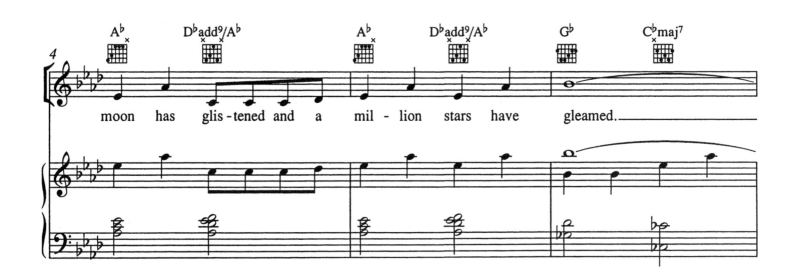

moon has glis-tened and a mil-lion stars have gleamed.

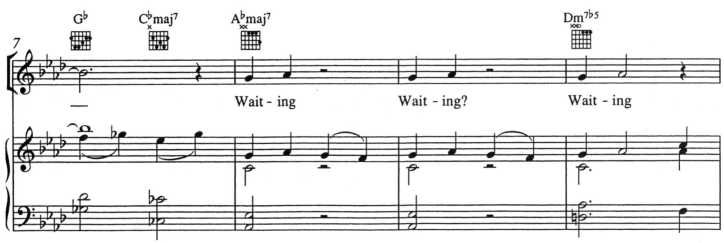

Wait-ing   Wait-ing?   Wait-ing

126

130

I Think I Like You - 8 - 7
24491

SAVE THE ANIMALS

Words and Music by
LESLIE BRICUSSE

SOMETHING IN YOUR SMILE

Words and Music by
LESLIE BRICUSSE

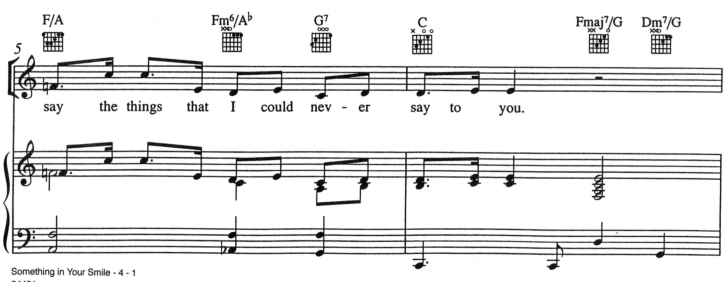

THE VOICE OF PROTEST

Words and Music by
LESLIE BRICUSSE

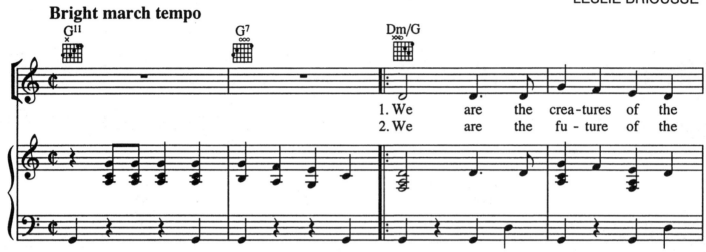

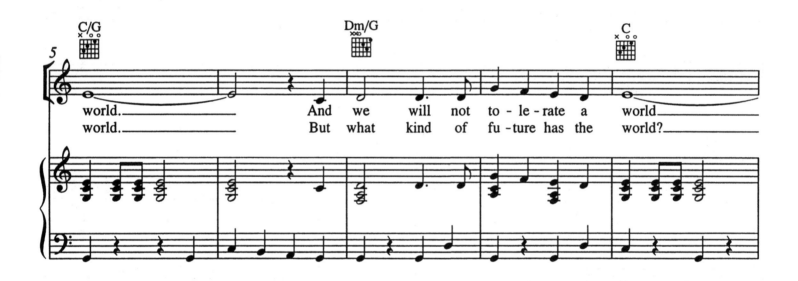

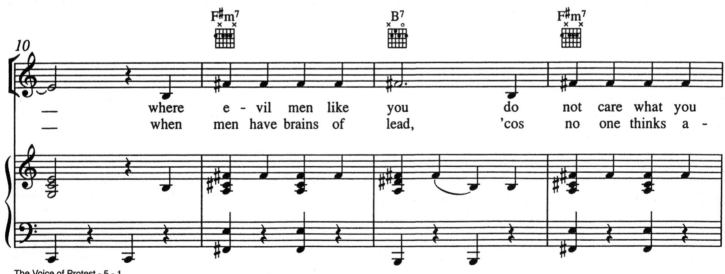

more voi - ces pro - test, 'til there's one voice of pro - test that's a roar. We shall make you mend your ways 'til the world sees bet - ter days, and we don't have to pro - test a - ny more. No we don't have to

PUDDLEBY-ON-THE-MARSH

Words and Music by
LESLIE BRICUSSE

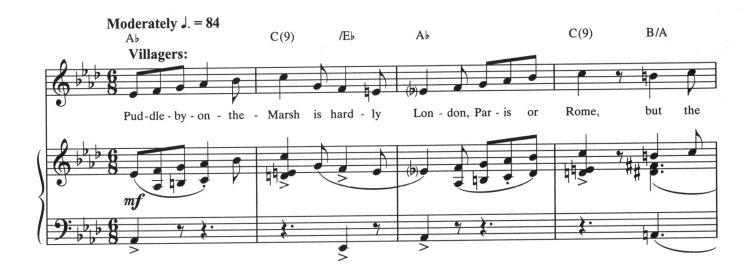

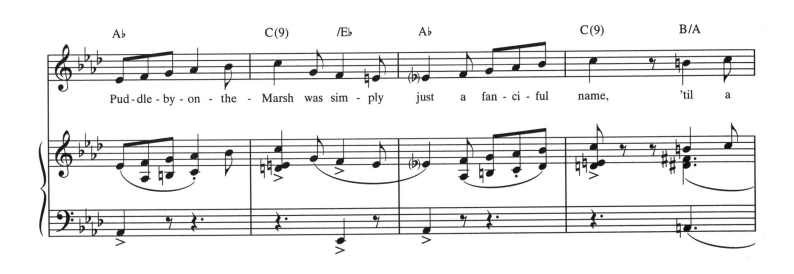

AT THE CROSSROADS

Words and Music by
LESLIE BRICUSSE

164

More freely (slightly faster)